When a Baby Is New

by Rosanne Keller
illustrated by Mark Fingar

New Readers Press
Publishing Division of Laubach Literacy International
Syracuse, New York

ISBN 0-88336-517-0

Cover design by Steve Rhodes

Revised 1989 by:
New Readers Press
Publishing Division of
Laubach Literacy International
Box 131, Syracuse, New York 13210
Printed in the United States of America
9 8 7 6 5 4 3 2

CONTENTS

Yelling Gets a Baby Strong

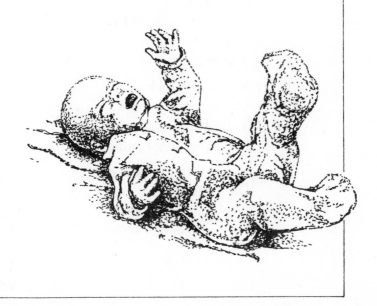

The baby yells

Lil and Bob are jumpy.
It is the baby.
The baby yells and yells!
And yells!
And yells!

Is the baby sick?
The baby is not sick.
Is the baby hungry?
The baby is not hungry.

Lil gives the baby a pat.
The baby yells.
Lil picks up the baby.
The baby yells.

Lil looks at Bob.
Bob looks at Lil.
The baby yells and yells!

Lil gives the baby to Bob.
The baby yells.
Bob puts the baby in the bed.
Bob has had it.
Bob yells, "This is a bad baby!"

Lil is hurt.
The baby yells and yells.

A baby is not bad

Lil and the baby are visiting Ann.
The baby is yelling.
Ann looks at Lil.
Ann says, "Is the baby wet?"

Lil yells, "The baby is not wet!
The baby is not hungry!
The baby is not sick!
The baby yells and yells and yells.
The baby is bad!"

Lil is mad.
Lil is sad.
Lil is hurting.

Ann gives Lil a pat.
Ann says, ''The baby is not bad.
A baby is a baby.
And a baby yells.''

''Look at the baby,'' Ann says.
''Yelling gets him kicking.
Yelling gets a baby strong.
Put the baby in the bed.
Let the baby yell.''

Yelling gets a baby strong

Ann gives Lil a cup of coffee.
Ann says, "A baby yells.
Mothers get mad.
Fathers get mad.
Mothers get sad.
Fathers get sad.
This is not bad."

Ann says, "Listen.
The baby is not yelling!"

Lil listens.
The baby is not yelling.
The baby is not yelling!

Ann says, "A baby yells.
The mother is hurt.
The father is hurt.
The baby is not hurt.
Yelling gets a baby strong."

Thanks for the baby

Bob comes in.
Bob puts his hand on Lil's neck.
Bob gives Lil a pat.

Bob listens.
Bob says, ''The baby is not yelling!''

Lil and Bob run to the baby.
The baby is in his bed.
The baby is kicking.
Hand in hand, Bob and Lil look at him.

Lil says, ''The baby is not bad.
A baby is a baby.
And a baby yells.
Yelling gets a baby strong.''

Bob pats Lil's hand.
Bob says, ''Thanks for this baby!''
Bob pats the baby.
The baby kicks and kicks.

Hugging Is Loving

Hugging is loving

Children need love.
Children need hugs and kisses.
When parents give love, children give love back.
Then parents and children are happy.

Children look at parents.
Children watch.
Children copy parents.
When parents love, children love back.
When parents hurt, children hurt back.
Children need love badly.
Children need hugs.

Mothers and fathers need hugs.
Children and parents need a lot of love.

Running and jumping with children is loving.
Kisses and laughs are loving.
Gifts and lunches and help are loving.
Telling funny things to children is loving.
Singing and rocking are loving.
Listening to children is loving.
Hugging is loving.

Hitting and yelling are not loving.
A person does not need hitting and yelling.
When a little person is hit and yelled at, it is hard
    for him to love.

When children live in love, children are happy.
When parents hit and yell, children turn from
    parents.
Children hit and yell.
When this happens, brothers and sisters are not
    happy.
The family is hurt.

But love fixes hurt.

Children need lots of things.
But of the things children need, love is at the top
    of the list.
Love is a gift parents can give.
Hugs, kisses, and laughs are gifts of love.
Hugging is loving.

A baby is afraid of falling

A baby is a very little person.
A baby needs lots of things.
A baby is afraid of lots of things.
One of the things a baby is afraid of is falling.
A baby is afraid she will fall.

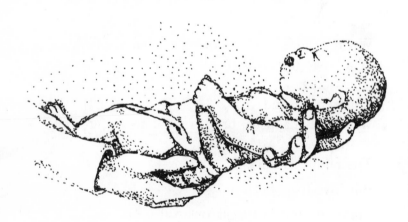

When a parent moves fast,
    the baby is afraid.
Her arms lift up.
Her legs jump.
The baby yells.
When a parent picks up a baby fast, the baby is
    afraid.
When a parent runs with the baby, the baby is
    afraid.
She is afraid she will fall.
When the parent puts the baby on her bed quickly,
    the baby is afraid she will fall.
When the parent does not hold the baby's head
    up, the baby is afraid.
The baby thinks the parent will drop her.

A baby needs to be covered well, in a small nest of
    covers.
She needs to be picked up and carried—not
    quickly, not hurried.
Then a baby is not afraid of falling.

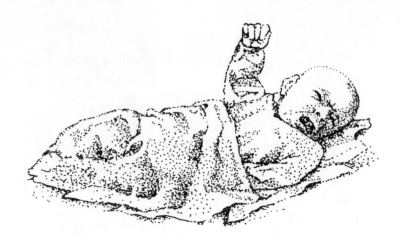

A baby is afraid of hunger

A baby is afraid of hunger.
The baby thinks hunger hurts.
The baby yells and yells when he is hungry.

A baby needs to be fed.
He needs to be fed often.
But he has other needs.

A baby needs love.
Love and feeding go with one another.
Love and feeding go hand in hand.

Pick up the baby.
Give him a hug.
Sing to him.
Sit with him in your arms when you feed him.
Feeding is loving.

A baby needs to be fed often.
A baby needs to be loved often.
Feeding starts with love.
Loving starts with feeding.

A baby is often afraid of hunger.
A baby is often afraid.
He needs to be fed, and he needs to be loved.
Love and feeding go hand in hand.

A baby is afraid of loud noises

Loud noises make a baby jump.
Loud noises make a baby afraid.
A baby is afraid of yelling.
A baby is afraid of banging.
A baby is afraid of lots of noises.

Pans banging in the kitchen make a baby afraid.
When mothers and fathers yell, a baby is afraid.
Children banging and jumping and yelling make a
    baby afraid.

When a loud noise makes a baby afraid, pick up
    the baby.
Give her a hug.
Carry her to the noise.
Let her look at what is making the noise.

Tell her what the noise is.
Tell her you love her.
Tell her not to be afraid.
Sing to her.
Rock her in your arms.
Then she will not be afraid.

A baby needs to sleep

A little baby needs lots of sleep.
A baby needs to sleep and sleep.
Some babies sleep a lot.
Some babies yell a lot.
Some parents think the baby does not think he
    needs sleep.
But the baby does need sleep.

Sleep helps a baby grow.
A baby needs to sleep often to grow.
He needs to be fed often to grow.
He needs to be loved often to grow.

Let the baby yell.
Yelling gets a baby strong.
He will stop yelling.
He will go to sleep.
A baby sleeps more than you think.

Tell the other children, "Shhhh. No noise. Let the
    baby sleep."

Then the parents can get some sleep.

Children are a gift of love

Children need lots of things.
Children need to be fed.
Children need to be watched.
Children need...and on and on and on.

But, the funny thing is, parents need children.
Parents need the little persons.
Parents put up with yells, and falls, and burns, and
  cuts, and doctors' checkups.
Parents put up with snakes, puppies, and mud
  and things in the kitchen.
Parents kiss hurts, hunt homework,
  rock, sing, pet, and hug.

Children help make a family.
And families are fun.

Parents need children.
Children need parents.
Parents and children need love.
Hugging is loving.
A happy family hugs a lot.

Something New:
Care of an Infant

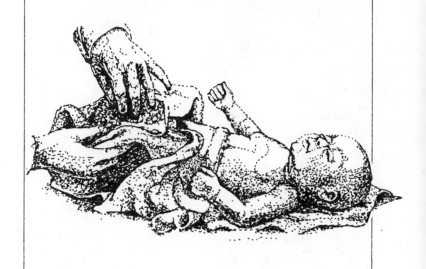

"I'm here!"

You can hold me.
You can feed me.
You can hear me!
You can look at me.
You can watch me grow.

A star is born!

Now what?!

Don't worry

I may be tiny.
I may be helpless.
I may scare you.
But
I'm tougher than you think!

I can cry **LOUD**
and long—

But crying does not hurt me.

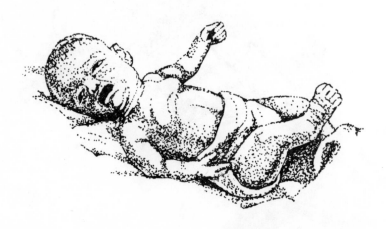

Just keep COOL.
I won't break.

Remember:

I have needs.
My needs are
—to be held
—to be dry
—to be clean
—to be warm
—to be fed
—to be able to sleep, sleep, sleep.

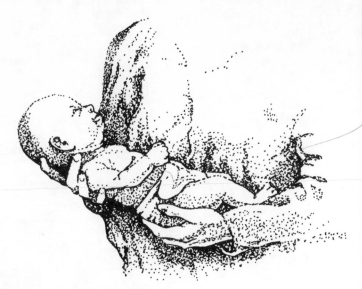

Holding a baby

Be gentle.
Be slow and easy.
No quick moves or loud noises.
Talk to the baby and tell her what you are going
   to do.

To lift up a baby

Slip one hand under her bottom.
Slip the other hand under her neck.
Spread your fingers.
Hold up the baby's head and shoulders.
Lift the baby slowly to your arms.

Football hold

When you hold a baby like a football, your other
   hand is free.
But watch out—don't bump the baby's head.

Cradle hold

This is best for feeding.
It is also cozy.
Be sure the baby's head
   rests in the bend of
   your arm.

Over-the-shoulder hold

This is best for burping.

**Remember: Support the baby's head, back,
   and bottom.**

Diapering a baby

You need

—a clean, folded cloth or paper diaper
—large safety pins (for cloth diapers only)
—paper tissues
—a warm, damp washcloth.

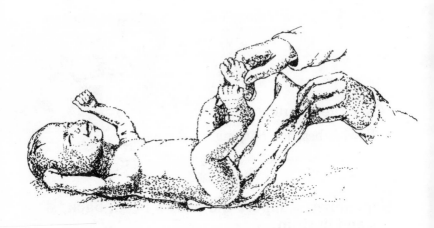

To change a diaper

Take off the wet or dirty diaper.
Put the dirty diaper in a diaper pail or garbage pail.

Wipe the baby's bottom with the damp washcloth.
Dry his bottom.
Put the clean diaper under his bottom.
Put the thick side of the diaper in front for boys and in
     back for girls.
Put the diaper on the baby.
If you use safety pins, slip your fingers between the
     baby and the diaper.

Keep safety pins out of the baby's reach.
Keep powders and lotions out of his reach.

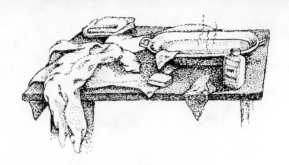

Bathing a baby

You need

- —a towel spread out on a table or counter
- —a tub of *warm* water
  (Test the water with your elbow.
  If it doesn't feel hot or cold, it's OK.)
- —a towel or two
- —a washcloth
- —clean clothes, a folded diaper, a blanket
- —a bar of baby soap.

To bathe the baby

Take the baby's clothes and diaper off.
Clean her bottom if it's dirty.
Wrap her snugly in a flannel blanket.
Use the football hold to carry her.

Be sure to support her head.

Test the water temperature.
Wash the baby's face, neck, and ears with the
    washcloth.

>   Don't rub hard.
>   No soap.
>   Dry the face, neck,
>   and ears.
>   Talk to her! Smile
>   at her!
>   Make the bath fun.

Keep the blanket wrapped snugly.
Hold the baby over the tub and gently wash her
    hair.
Use baby soap.

Careful: Don't slop water in her eyes.

Test the water again.
Take the blanket off the baby.
Slowly put her in the tub.
Talk to her!
Sing to her!

Remember to support her head.

Soap your free hand.
Wash the baby's arms, chest, and hands.
Rinse the soap off.

Soap your free hand again.
Wash her tummy, genitals, legs, and feet.
Rinse the soap off.

Lean her forward across your free arm.
With your wrist under her chest, grasp her arm.
Soap your other hand.
Wash her back and bottom.
Rinse the soap off.

**Never leave the baby alone in the water or on
the table.**

Then lift the baby out of the tub.
Lay her on the towel on the table.
Wrap her snugly in another towel.

Hold her close.
Rock her.
Sing to her.
Talk to her as you pat her dry.

Now put her back on the dry towel on the table.
Wrap her in the dry towel or blanket.

There is nothing like a clean baby.

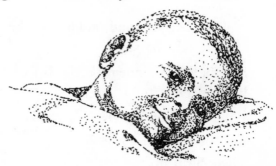

Dressing a baby

You need

—clean clothes for the baby
—folded diaper
—diaper pins
—undershirt
—blanket.

To dress the baby

Put the diaper on the baby.

Put the undershirt on the baby.
Slip your fingers through the wrist end of the
    sleeve.
Pull the baby's hand, holding all his fingers,
    through the sleeve.

Put the suit or gown on the baby.
If the neck is tight, stretch it out.

Wrap the baby snugly in a blanket.
Put the baby in his bed.

Then clean up the bath things.

Feeding a baby

You need

—a bottle of formula or milk
—a bottle warmer or a small pan of hot water

OR

(if the baby is old enough)

—baby cereal
—jars of food
—a small spoon
—a bottle warmer or a small pan of hot water.

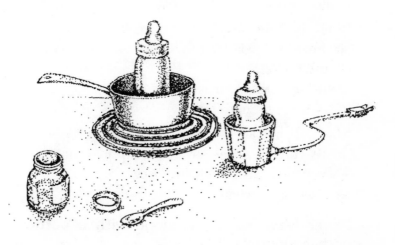

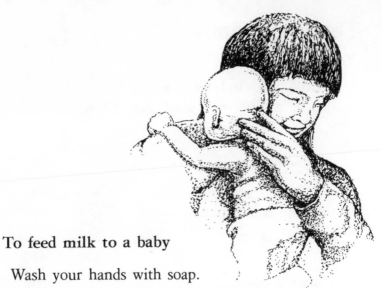

To feed milk to a baby

Wash your hands with soap.

Warm the bottle.
Test it by sprinkling a drop of milk on your wrist.
It should not feel hot or cold.

Wrap the baby snugly in a blanket.
Sit down in a comfortable chair with the baby and
    the bottle.
Hold the bottle so it is not pressing her mouth.
Relax. Enjoy. Sing. Talk.

When about half the milk is gone, lean the baby
    on your shoulder, or sit her up in your lap.
Then gently pat or rub her back.
Do this again when the bottle is finished.

**Never leave an infant alone with a bottle in
her mouth.**

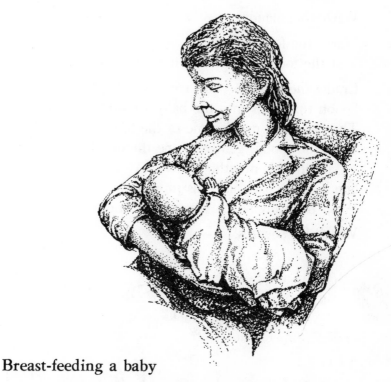

Breast-feeding a baby

Many mothers nurse (breast-feed) their babies.
To nurse a baby, you need a mother, a baby, and
a comfortable chair.

To give a baby solid food

Wash your hands.

Warm the food.
Test the food by touching it to your lip.

Cradle the baby in your arm.
Spoon tiny bites into the baby's mouth.
The baby will drool some of the food.
With the spoon, gently scrape the drools and oozes
    around his mouth.
Spoon them back into his mouth.
Wash the baby's face when he is finished.

Watch for sneezes!

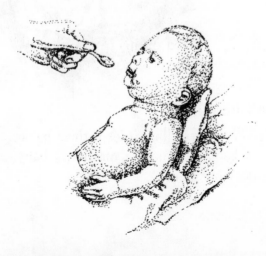

After the baby has eaten...
and **BURPED**

Gently put him to bed on his tummy.
Cover him with a warm blanket.
Turn off the light.
Then let him sleep.

Clean up the bottles and dishes.

What to do if the baby cries

and cries

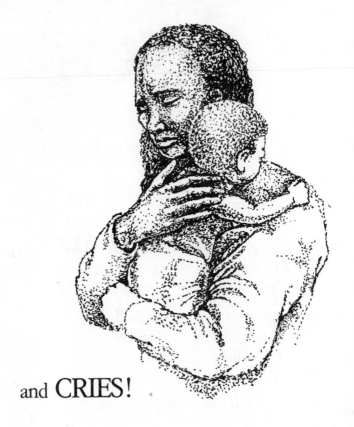

and CRIES!

Change her diaper.
Feed her.
Turn her over.
Rock her.
Sing to her.
Talk to her.
Make sure she is warm enough—or cool enough.

But sometimes, nothing seems to help!

Maybe the baby just needs to be alone.
We all have our bad days!

A baby needs

—to be held
—to be dry
—to be clean
—to be warm (but not too warm)
—to be fed
—to sleep and sleep.

But mostly . . .

A baby needs to be

LOVED!

A little life is in your hands.